ALSO BY JOHN ASHBERY

POETRY

Some Trees

The Tennis Court Oath

Rivers and Mountains

The Double Dream of Spring

Three Poems

The Vermont Notebook

Self-Portrait in a Convex Mirror

Houseboat Days

As We Know

Shadow Train

A Wave

Selected Poems

April Galleons

Flow Chart

Hotel Lautréamont

And the Stars Were Shining

Can You Hear, Bird

Wakefulness

The Mooring of Starting Out

FICTION

A Nest of Ninnies

(with James Schuyler)

PLAYS

Three Plays

CRITICISM

Reported Sightings: Art Chronicles 1957–1987

GIRLS ON THE RUN

GIRLS ON THE RUN

A POEM BY

JOHN ASHBERY

FARRAR, STRAUS AND GIROUX • NEW YORK

Farrar, Straus and Giroux
19 Union Square West, New York 10003

Copyright © 1999 by John Ashbery
All rights reserved
Distributed in Canada by Douglas & McIntyre Ltd.
Printed in the United States of America
Designed by Jonathan D. Lippincott
First published in 1999 by Farrar, Straus and Giroux
First paperback edition, 2000

Parts of this poem have appeared in *The Germ*, *Grand Street*, *Lingo*, *Modern Painters*, *On Paper*, and *Shiny*.

Library of Congress Cataloging-in-Publication Data
Ashbery, John.
  Girls on the run : a poem / by John Ashbery.—1st ed.
    p.   cm.
  ISBN 0-374-52697-4 (pbk.)
  1. Darger, Henry, 1892–1972—Adaptations.   2. Girls—Poetry.
I. Title
PS3501.S475G57   1999
811'.54—dc21   99–18682

To Eugene, Rosanne, and Joseph

GIRLS ON THE RUN

GIRLS ON THE RUN

after Henry Darger

I

A great plane flew across the sun,
and the girls ran along the ground.
The sun shone on Mr. McPlaster's face, it was green like an elephant's.

Let's get out of here, Judy said.
They're getting closer, I can't stand it.
But you know, our fashions are in fashion
only briefly, then they go out
and stay that way for a long time. Then they come back in
for a while. Then, in maybe a million years, they go out of fashion
and stay there.
Laure and Tidbit agreed,
with the proviso that after that everyone would become fashion
again for a few hours. Write it now, Tidbit said,
before they get back. And, quivering, I took the pen.

Drink the beautiful tea
before you slop sewage over the horizon, the Principal directed.
OK, it's calm now, but it wasn't two minutes ago. What do you want me to
　　do, said Henry,
I am no longer your serf,
and if I was I wouldn't do your bidding. That is enough, sir.
You think you can lord it over every last dish of oatmeal
on this planet, Henry said. But wait till my ambition
comes a cropper, whatever that means, or bursts into feathered bloom
and burns on the shore. Then the kiddies dancing sidewise
declared it a treat, and the ice-cream gnomes slurped their last that day.

Inside, in the twilit nest of evening,
something was coming undone. Dimples could feel it,
surging over her shoulder like a wave of energy. And then—
it was gone. No one had witnessed it but herself.
And so Dimples took off for the city, which was near and wholesome.
There, with her sister Larissa, she planned the big blue boat
that future generations will live in, and thank us for. It twitched
at its steely moorings, and seemed to say: Live, like life, with me.

Let the birds wash over them, Laure said, for what use are earmuffs
in a snowstorm, except to call attention to distant tots
who have strayed. And now the big Mother warms them,
accepts them, for the nervous predicates they are. Far from the beach-
　　fiend's
howling, their adventure nurses itself back
to something like health. On the fifth day it takes a little blancmange
and stands up, only to fall back into a hammock.
I told you it was coming, cried Dimples, but look out,

4

Another big one is on the way!
And they all ran, and got out, and that was that for that day.

I I

Hungeringly, Tidbit approached the crone who held the bowl,
. . . drank the honey. It had good things about it.
Now, pretty as a moment,
Tidbit's housecoat sniffed the undecipherable,
the knowable past. They were anxious
to get back to work. Diane was looking relaxed.
Then, some say, Pete said
it was the afternoon backing up again, inexorable
with dreams, looking for garbage to pick a fight with.
"My goodness! Do you suppose his blowhole's . . . ?"

Sometime later they returned with Pete and the others,
he all excited, certain he had spotted a fuse this time.
Rags the mutt licked and yelped. "Oh, get down!"
But Rags seemed to be on to something. "And if they come
through the alfalfa this time, we'll have a nice idea
of where they are, of who these men are. If they abrade
the abandoned silo, no one will be wiser. Look, their pastel
tent, and flags made from the same substance, waving *dehors*—
I've got to get an angle on this, a firm tack of some kind."
Willingly, the flood washed over the day
and so much that was complicated, from the past:
the tiny doggy door Rags had made with a T-square,
surplus sequins.

And if they don't want to play
according to our rules, what then? "Why, then
we'll come up with something, like the sink-drain.
Anyway, this is all just an excuse for you to leave your posts,
toying with anagrams, while the real message
is being written in the stars. To go ahead,
it says, but be watchful for scouts
in the corn shocks. This close to Halloween there are lots of little bumps
around, and tea cosies to shroud them. Beware one last time;
but as the spirit of going is to go, I can't
control you, advise you much longer. Just keep on
persevering, and then we'll know what we have done matters most
    to us."
        With that, the sticks uprooted the tent.
A thousand passions came unleashed,
but fortunately for the girls, none of them were around to witness it—
they were off in a cage with the canaries.
                        Now, though,
when it came time to vote for who the deed was done
by, the others mattered too. It was just their pot luck.

Oh well, Laure offered, we were going to close down that shaftway
anyway, and the subway came close: It was Mother and her veering
playthings again, torn between the impossible alternatives of existing
and saying no to menace. To everyone's surprise the bus stopped.
Our stalwart little band of angels got on it, and were taken for a ride
into the next chapter, a dim place of curlicues and bas-reliefs.
If I had a handle, Laure thought.

Out in Michigan, or was it Minnesota, though, time had stopped
to see what it could see, which wasn't much. A recent hooligan scare had
    blighted the landscape,
lowering the temperature by several degrees. "Having
to pee ruins my crinoline relentlessly,
because it comes only ecstatically."
But the wounded cow knew otherwise.
                                She was at least sixty,
had many skins covering her own, regal one. So then they all cry,
at sea. The lawnmower is emitting sparks again,
one doesn't know how many, or how much faster it will have to go
to meet us at the Denizens' by six o'clock. We'd have been better
off letting the prisoners stage their own war. Now I don't know
so much, and with Aunt Jennie at my side we could release
a few more bombs and not know it.
                                Everywhere in the tangled schist
someone was living, it seemed to say, this is my doing;
whoever shall come afterward is a delusion. And I went round
the corner to say, Well it sure looks like an improvement—hey,
why don't you tie your shoes, and then your bonnet will be picture-
    perfect?

No, only getting away
has any value to her: A stone's throw is better than a mile
since one will have to be up again much later, and this way
saves time. How often did you let your mother say,
How did you get your Sundays packed away? And yet it's always
    treasonable
to be in the middle. H'm, there are objections to that,

just as I thought. This might help. Yes. But the color
of this paint is too fabulous, I'd asked for something fragmented
like sea-spray. In that case we cannot be of service to you. Farewell.

Now I had walked the terrible byways for what seemed like too long.
Now another was following, insensately.
Would there be foodstuffs on the steps? How did that ladder point into
    nowhere?
"Shuffle, you miser!" Just so, Shuffle said,
I don't want to be around when the gang erupts
into centuries of inviolate privilege, and cisterns tumble down
the side of the slope, and all is gone more or less naturally to hell.
To which Dimples replied, Why not? Why not just give yourself, one time,
to the floods of human resources that are our day?
Because I don't want to live at an angle to the blokes who micromanage
our territory, that's all. Oh, who do you mean? Why, the red-trimmed
    zebras,
Shuffle said, that people thinks is the cutest damn things in town
until the victory bonfire on the square, and then there's more racing
and chasing than you can shake a banjo-string at,
and it'll have muddled you over by the time the war has crested.

He sat, eating a cheese sandwich, wondering if it would be his last,
fiddled and sank away.
                    And as far as the wires
could stretch, into the inevitable jerk-kingdom, the little girl
crawled on her hands and feet. That was no jack-in-the-box
back there, that was the real thing.

                    *   *   *

Yes, Stuart Hofnagel, they came to you, they'd expected big things
of you back in Arkadelphia, and now you were a soured loner like
    anybody.
Old town, you seem to remember otherwise.
That was you backing into love, wasn't it? So we all came and were glad
    that day.
That was all a fine day for us. Happiness, that we loved you so much;
phony energy, because we were happy.
Yet the town held back, rinsing her skirts
in the dour brook that fled the sawmill, just before four o'clock.
None of us slaves knew any different, having been nursed into solitude the
    night before last.
Certainly, if someone knocks on the open door
we will be pleasant, and look after the stranger just as if he were one of
    our own.
That's the way we were made. We can't help it. Conversely,
if a friend obtrudes his thinking into this plan of ours,
we shall deny all knowledge of him. It happens this way in the wilderness.
Plus the pot is full of old oddments. The rhubarb stains on Peggy's frock
almost—but not quite—match its rickrack trim.
That's where the human aspect comes in.
Some were born to play with, to think constantly about it, with a nod,
not much more, to the future and what its executives might have in store.
We aren't easily intimidated.
And yet we are always frightened,
frightened that this will come to pass
and we all unable to do anything about it, in case it ever does.
So we appeal to you, sun, on this broad day.
You were ever a helpmate in times of great churning, and fatigue.
You make us forget how serious we are
and we dance in the lightning of your rhythm like demented souls
on a hospital spree. If only,

9

when the horse crawls up your back, you had known to make more of it.
But the climate is military, and yet one can't see too far ahead.
Better a storehouse of pearls than this battered shoehorn
of wood, yet it can cause everything to take place and change for you.

IV

Dearest, we had waited for this star,
the marriage couldn't take place without it. A louse
drags its lonely way up to the end of a porcupine quill, expires,
and can we have heard anything? I mean the paced breathing just
    outdoors,
and then inside, it's just squalid and quiet,
nothing more. I have a bowl of cherry syrup.

These halls, when the rush of spring is echoing, far ahead,
collapse into tendrils, their décor foreseen
since the dawn of history. One can walk across them, and time suddenly
seems funny, stops, is dead, or mute. And prisoners come begging
for a primrose, or a shaft of sunlight, and the all-seeing sees them
and averts his gaze until tomorrow. Thus, our doom, ringing with half-
    realized
fantasies, is a promise of a new beginning on another continent.
Only, we must get out of here. A man stands by a cactus, counting
the flecks of rage as they pass by, and you are in another suit,
abashed, a dapper salesman today. And the volley of the shooting gallery
vies with the welter of jarred complacencies, multiple over time,
if time wishes: "*Lacrimoso*, our sport is behind us!
Lacrimoso, we can't get anything done!
Lacrimoso, the bear has gone after the honey!

Lacrimoso, the honey drips incessantly
from the bough of a tree."

Worse, it was traditional to feel this way.

V

Just as a good pianist will adjust the piano stool
before his recital, by turning the knobs on either side of it
until he feels he is at a proper distance from the keyboard,
so did our friends plan their day. Sometimes, after a leisurely breakfast,
they would get to work immediately, cutting, gluing, stitching
as the model came entrancingly into view. Other days it was more of a
    pain,
or more elaborate. Persnickety Peggy was frequently at the heart of things,
her strength often an inspiration to the others, though offset by her
    tendency to brawl
and generally make a nuisance of herself. The other girls took this in
    stride,
though. Little by little the house was rising
where only sky had hung before, and it seemed like good news,
a good berth. That was before Tommy took over
and ruined everything. But I am getting ahead of my story.

Sometimes to wake up in the morning was enough. They began feeling
    better.
Lecture plans were discussed, and a gleaming white envelope, shocking in
    its purity
as the dawn, would be sealed by two or three of them. There,

that's better, no one would say, and that's how they got down to business.
On rainy days they would stay indoors
watching the chase of drops on the pane, realizing, a little half-frugally,
how it would be impossible to ever go outside. Moss drips on moss;
the more interesting-smelling exhibits have been packed away.
Or was there a terminus, sadly, deep underground? This, only children
    can know,
and some adults who have turned the steep corner into childhood.
Plums are ripening,
the pitcher of sangria darkens and deepens. So it was ever this way,
until it was past time to become "normal" again. Tell it to the neutered
    pets
that day! Already the verandas are awash with trouble, and color, the darts
    seldom miss their mark.
Heidi and Peter dissolve in the crystal furnace;
something says it's too late to change, now better to let it come toward
us, then we will see what it is made of.
To have had a son back there . . .
But the unthinkable is common knowledge now. We must let down a
    ladder
so the others may attach their boats to it, and in that way we shall be
    saved.
Only I think we're . . . It's all coming nearer.

VI

Nov. 7. Returned again to the exhibition. How strange it is that when we
least imagine we are enjoying themselves, a shaft of reason will bedazzle
us. Then it's up to us, or at any rate them, to think ourselves out of the
muddle and in so doing turn up whole again on the shore, impeached by a

sigh, so that the whole balcony of spectators goes whizzing past, out of
control, on a collision course with destiny and the bridesmaids' sobbing.
Of course, we listened, then whistled, and nobody answered, at least it
seemed nobody did. The silence was so intense there might have been a
sound moving around in it, but we knew nothing of that. Then we came
to. The pictures are so nice on the walls, it seems one might destroy
something by even looking at them; the tendency is to ignore by walking
around the partition into a small, cramped space that is flooded with
daylight. And what if we asked for another spoonful? Look, it's down
there, down at the bottom of the well, and we are no wiser for it, if
anybody asked. Which they don't. By common consent,
including ours, we are ignored and given the cold shoulder to. OK, so it's
all until another day, and we can see quite clearly into the needle whose
        thread is
waving slowly back and forth like a caterpillar, accomplishing its end.
So may it be until the end that is eternity.

VII

The thread ended up on the floor,
where threads go.
It became a permanent thing, like silver—
every time you polish it, a little goes away.
Then the ducks arrived, it was raining.
Such a lot of going around and doing!
Sometimes they were in sordid sexual situations;
at others, a smidgen of fun would intrude on our day
which exists to be intruded on, anyway.
Its value, to us, is incommensurate
with, let's say, the concept of duration, which kills,

surely as a serpent hiding behind a stump.
Our phrase books began to feel useless—for once
you have learned a language, what is there to do but forget it?
An illustration changes us.

These were cloistered. They stayed
with us that winter, then went on awhile.
Soon they were back. It was partially time to go out in the opening.
Some enjoyed it.
Then, if they were true,
the blue rabbit heaped bones upon them. There was no going back,
now, though, some did go back. Those who did
didn't get very far. The others came out a little ahead,
I think . . . I'm not sure.

Look, this is what I am, what I'm made of.
Am I then to usurp the rose
that blows on time's pediment, wrapping all wisps in a kind of bundle
of awe? But the sundial smiled in the rain, the stile
beckoned, the sign said it was three miles. In the lane the parson's
ambulance pestered gold pigtails, who were in for a shock
when the fox returned smiling, fanning his great tail in the comet
of the lighthouses the sausages were so concerned about.
Did the game of stealing please any? Here, on the other side, they were in
    sync,
their bowls of muesli crooning to the sidelong bats of evening, and then
    they were let out
to smoke a cigarette in the meadow. No one knew how many
tried to escape, or how many were successful. You had to read it
in the evening's news, and by then sea-cows were weary.
They taxed themselves out of existence. Our raft capsized

and they opined the day was bright with promise, though shut off
from what really happened. It was time for golf.

This was that day's learning.

Finally when Angela could retrieve her moorings they sent the tide out,
but it came back next day, increasingly bizarre.
Bunny and Philip weren't sure they wanted to see more. "But you must,"
Angela urged, breathing a little faster. Then they all wanted to know why
    it goes on
all the time, and the preacher answered it was due to bats. In the silos. Oh,
I thought you wanted to know, Philip said. We do, but other than you there
    are two
pails formally, and no one can figure out what is inside. Indeed? Well I'll
take the plunge, Philip volunteered. He was always a brave little kid.
Now it was this side of sunset again. Nobody knew which was in error: the
    stove, or its corset.
After which the elm buds chanced a summer intrusion
and all the nifty year was almost gone. Well isn't that a catastrophe, Aunt
    Clara gurgled,
or are some of you please going to take it outside? Aw, but it's raining,
    someone grumbled,
why can't we stay inside and have school?
Yes but the quitter must go far out into the bogs. It's time for the badgers
    to nest
and who is that coming over the hill this time? It's
Spider, Angela suggested.

But as for leaving you all without a tale to tell, I would be daft,
nay derelict, not to insist on where the others have gone. Isn't there a place

to stop, that we'll all know about when we come to it?
Yes there is, she said, we'll just all have to back down
into the gloom, and bait our hooks with peanut butter.
Which is what they did
and so they left home that day.

VIII

"All aboard! If there's one thing I hate it's a loner,"
Uncle Philip said, or someone who's beside himself. Please, Uncle,
can't we go out today? Aw, shut up, Philip said. Now there were two bald
      uncles
who lived in the nearby swamp. One of them knew Shuffle. And he said:
If it's to play in, why not. But if it's just to play over and around
then I don't see why you need to, and indeed shall expend every effort
to see that you don't. But if the mirror
refract any of this, then boy you can be sure you can go.
And in a little while the mirror reflected all of them
back at each other. This was exceptional. Those getting up to leave were
      stayed
in their rubber boots, and those arriving were perplexed and pleasured.
      Why, isn't
it a rebus, Aunt Clara wondered, and Tootles agreed that it was.
From a distant patch of loam the speck started arriving, bigger
with each hulking gasp. Why doesn't the foreman go, someone wondered,
      it's
part of his job description, and the others can go anyway, if they want to.
      So all
got to be sensitized. And in the large gap for brooding that was created
some of the saner heads got wind of the passing football

and were mortified into a decision. Sun shovel it in,
there's no more room for today, and you can go. I said you can go.
Oh, the man said, not understanding, and a third time they shouted at
    him:
You can go.
And he betook himself on his two legs.

Under frozen mounds of yak butter the graffiti have their day, and are
    elaborate,
some say. Nobody wants to go there. Yes, she said, we will swim
there if necessary. The arroz con pollo can take us
and do with us what we will. Just as I thought I had found a solution
to this and other present error, the knitting needles collapsed.
Never bathe or shave on a cloudy day, Uncle Margaret cautioned. The
    twins were in limbo
over this but we steered the car carefully, permanently
toward them and they too were saved. Hey,
we put it all aside for a rainy day, and this is one, and this is just superior,
Dave asserted. And all we've got to do is roll over
and the dream will be over. Not so fast, Aunt Clara indicated, the gum
trees are a-rattle. The stealth of the horizon
nears us. That cat is asleep. And who shall take the dinner pail out
to the sodden farmhands, and just leave? Be it us,
that will be all OK. And in two strokes it was done. And they came and
    cancelled
the signature, so that everything was as it had been before. The militia
    capsized
and died from eating a certain kind of mold. Now the sentry wanes,
sinks and dies of its own weight. All the marbles have rolled inside the
    house.

IX

And now everyone must sleep.
The kiddies are silent for a while.

and yes, singly or in pairs,
they come down to the water's edge, to drink their fill. The wide-eyed
    pansies gaze
immutably. Rev up the old flivver, we'll be disparate for a time
and then we'll see, the mice will see. Why all the fuss?
You know you came here just for this, this kiss, on the face, the dog said.
Where are you starting to go? Are my pants too wide?
What if someone else on the other side of the globe
told you this, would he fall off? Would I?
That's why they say stand clear.
You can never do yourself favors enough, in the rosebush
from which man never extricates himself. I see,
someone said. Does it matter about being alone? No it's important
but not that important. I see, this person said. But then what if I am
no longer alone? What then? Two of you can board as long as one stays on
    the lookout,
the relaxed policeman said. He brought a sandwich down the street
and placed it on the curb, he was so nice. We didn't expect the birches
to explode just then. The sound traveled over the neighboring hills
down to the makeshift waterfront, lugubrious in the darkening air.
It's the cold
again he said. Every time I forget something, whenever anything is in
    motion
again, this happens, and I am not prepared for it. I'm plum scared.
Then you should go out,
your dress will be as morning to the cows,
she said. And he did and it was.

By and by Allen told us of a scheme
to rescue Pliable, if the latter consented, which surely he would,
and it would all seem as if it had never been.
But it would have, we'd know that, and ever after, as adults,
wandering the velveteen streets, we'd come upon someone who would have
    known someone
who wasn't all there and we'd be back at square one in the love market
and oceans of tremors would have been discovered. A word
would issue from a crack in the pavement, and it was up to Jane and the
    detective to decide
whether they'd heard it. If they hadn't, fine.
Otherwise it's down to the station
to sort everything out in the middle of the night, and not taken to too
    kindly
either. Drunks passed back and forth. Jane
was titillated but squeamish. She thought of asking Cupid
if the seams of her stockings were straight, but Pliable intervened
    strenuously,
arguing that no two people can take love into their own hands.
Oh. Excuse me. Bye bye. I'm
outta here. No, said Jane, you don't
understand, he means to be nice. He's a sheep, really. Yes but I don't see
how that affects me, and anyway I'm not interested. Oh, please, you must
    be,

she agitated, just for a little while as we perch
on this twig that must be the end of the world for us. Jolly good,
Pliable thought, it's me or you, now or never and here comes—

I awoke from the dream. A big boom
was passing over my head. I could see clear up the mizzen, if that counts,

any more, your honor, I just want to say I respects
all what is good, and don't come here any more, I won't. That is good.
We'll take off and be back pronto. Don't
answer the telephone until dawn. Supposing they come and
want to ask you and we are gone, or in the middle of something? That's
    OK but don't
be gone too long. We'll come too.

I'm no expert but I see a problem here.
The fisheries have come undone, as the headlong race to the pole
has made alarmingly evident. As I say, I can speak only for myself,
but as soon as I got here the rules became different.
They didn't apply to me any more, or to anyone else except a distant runt,
almost invisible in its litter. So how was
I to know who to stand up to, when to turn abrasive, when all things
    nestled,
equidistant, all hearts were charming, and it was good to be natural and
    sincere?
True, we had much to worry about,
other things to think about, but when has mankind had the leisure
to distract himself from these and other unassailable syllogisms?
So the truth just washed up on the shore,
a bundle of nerves, not resembling much of anything
we cared to remember. Was polite, stoical,
and anything else to deflect attention from its seething ambiguity.
It was time to come back, back into the flower-bedecked house.
A stunning moment of certainty survived
briefly, then it too was washed away in the rising flood,
tortured, unambitious.
School was over,
not just for that day but forever and for seasons to come.

The reason was that the truth was just average
on the iniquity scale, and nobody wanted to get involved.

X

Often a strange desire:
we hear you
you hear me
we can hear you
you make my period rounder.
You are the center of the universe
a tuber time invents.
We were all passing the fumes
of the car,
green sky explains
more tomorrow
under whatever sun they send up
to be worshipped,
imbibed,
glee from head to toe.
It will not do
and it's true I do
we had to have summer.
We were too baked.
Some of us got up to go,
the others stayed behind
in what position one wants to know.
Larry Sue said bye bye.
The sets of vigorous twins left by the walkway.
This is a nice place we're in.

Then it all comes to nothing walking
have you a care where we're walking.

Often a strange desire
mingles cats and near-greatness
that you all left startled standing. There are no more heaters
    understandably.
A pipe is needed, pleasant moments.
Heaven knows the place of our desires—
it is here somewhere, over there
or under this.
We must add up as many to the total
as is possible. To the passing fine day
were added the rudiments of music.
I too a cruel one I gave some
of my substance to the wind
and then it returned it I came ashore.
I am overly satisfied with the present-day facility.
Are you Pam's nursery arrangement.
No four of them insisted count the dogs. Count the dogs!
Count the dogs as furniture
as otherwise there will be no chairs.
No warrant out for his arrest I see no
other way I came down the stairs in darkness
to what is here.
In darkness we live sensibly perhaps satisfied with too much.
But when daylight wanes we take aim
at a larger quadrant. There are people in the store.
There is a sale of fine foods and beaded hair products.
So notice this gun lest you withdraw altogether from chiming.
He was infinitely dark and creepy
but at a point leaving for the sun state it is hard not to get off

not to leave this train that takes us with it as long as we want it to go.

I was looking at a book he created, glued and spliced.

Next the decorations are kablooey, old potted bricks.

He took a couple of puffs.

Plastic star removal continues.

Our reporter took an immigration ride, the dented land seemed there. By all accounts something was "obtuse."

We must have spent half on vegetables the fertilizer crop was good.

Old Mr. Jenkins liked to play around with himself in that way.

The place has to

be there I had to recognize it.

Do you like clams Emily no not raw steamed.

Those look softer. I still like 'em.

Instead of letting it be area in all those big air bubbles—

rubber.

They were so . . . impatient.

After I jiggled it back and forth the finish started coming off in my hand.

Oh it's a song something to sing.

In my head we sang under

the vanilla tree

where breasts are stacked loosely.

Why should American tourists interrogate the town hall.

The justices file in file their brief their file

soon it is time to go to bed for dinner.

The obelisk hobbled over. "Do you know which way

to the basilica?" he marveled.

Such tall spruces and so many of them!

I had foreseen everything but this

in this place of spruces whether they be right

or not they have a right to be here

I guess or I try not to think it.

It is a nursery ditty grave or gay.
It seems to say
how much longer will my spruces be on tap?
How many more years of availability?
Wisely the spruces contented themselves with rustling.
It was just like a kitchen with the blue gas burning
in a special flame for all to see.
So all grew. The tainted fir-trees
fell over and were loam. All were.
We can see enough on this side to convince us of the merit of that other.
But if a tank wishes to convince us we cannot contradict that.
So all grew, more and more, into the bower of empowerment,
and all were pursued by what happened this time
so as not to be puzzled by what happened next on the long pier
of time reaching to the vanishing point.

Some were cold, some were near, some were clear.
Some were like lighthouses out of which startled gulls flew
to change something in the colored environment of sky
before retracing their steps to the dome.
Some of them were having kittens that night;
it changed something for everybody
and not enough to come out on top, oh well
the seer said my pastry is here.
I shall dispose of myself as I will
and I shall not come back
and no one will notice not ever not even the dimpled sun
as it coasts majestically by these geese
that come up short. In good time
I shall return for I have other things to do other fish to fry
he said but in the meantime it will look as though I'm not coming back
or returning. The woods resounded with campers' cries,

they are bringing something back, back to the deck
with them. "You see I should never have gone away,"
the seer remarked, now I can not ever
as long as accounts not be settled and the ride over the corn is over.
It seemed as though shale were about to break off the Old Man of the
    Mountain.
The holidays mystify me I cannot grow
as long as that path undulates in front of me,
and that crow ululates devaluating me
within the radius of this embroidery frame for ever and ever,
where "pie are square" and nobody knows how many.
Ssh, you are loud.
The seer teeters on the bench near the pool.
It is all just about over.
A fine man with coal nostrils
he was just about ready for this fix
when April surprised us with mistrials.
The man gone again, triumphant
in his absence
and with some remainder of light, of permanency
sliding toward day. I feel

that this is a letter being delivered to me, haply at dusk before night's
    purple
wrinkles have shifted the scenery, perhaps dolorously into death and the
    storm-
tinged future of lying and social regret. Don't stand, I might see you there,
she said. Helpless but doomed,

he countered good-humoredly. And these are our intuitions!

XI

First the cellos rebelled. Then a broader breaking-out erupted
nearer to home. All the girls were paralyzed (for a minute)
but Jenny Wren came to release them from the spell
Tom Cat had caused. They ran away, glad for that day.
Until Bruin came home and lay with his big amazing paws
on the hooked rug and it was time to go again. Goodbye,
Bruin said. I'll see you in the piece of country next door
which is exactly what happened, behind the tattered gate.
Then it was almost time to go fishing again. Here they paused,
wondering whether any of them had seen the big flash in the sky.
They decided to go no further. The tree dropped its seeds
into the birdbath. Alas the long wall, for all under this spell
will be ungrown some day, and are still here
to kiss the stair. Never mind, they said,
we'll all be here to cheer you on, and then they didn't mind.
Some had come unconvinced about the importance
of this daydream in which they were all entombed. Hark, one said, it
    smells like ice
or night here. Another agreed. They looked down on the procession
of sad children imagining they'd been forgotten about, and one stood in
    strength
on a tire rim and blew a whistle to the others. Zounds, it's our escape
one said. Here in the city repugnant with dust, Pliable's house was on fire
and nobody knew to stop it. I'll wager it was arson, Kitty said,
and others fervently agreed. He was coming back with a big sack
on his back, filled with plunder, perhaps, but there was no time to think of
    roses.
They had all walked for the day. Tonight's
question mark loomed in the agate sky, pointing them toward dewdrops
and madness. Are you listening, one of them said,

or just insane. Look, this pulley works,
we'll unscrew the pears from the plate, and put them back again,
and no one will ever know the difference. So they set to work, with a right
    good will,
saw and hammer in hand, and little by little the thing took shape.

It was the exact replica of a house
Tim had seen in his travels. Be it blue,
or red, I'll have it, Pliable said. Yes but you must go out
into the wind, one said, it's not that easy to see. I'll
wager I see it, he said. In fact she had achieved her level.
Ten million visitors are anticipated
next season, and as for the future, who knows
what it holds? They let down the bar
and each traveler was safely enclosed for the night.
It couldn't have been that anyone was coming to have it
or Bill the barrel would have known. For which everyone
was thankful, and induced into sleep, but
with a terrifying roar the house exploded again.
Now let me sink into my minutest crevices
if ever I give up a latchkey again! Yet girls and boys rolled
on together, the end was not in sight,
nor was it a division yet. Thanks, the cowboy yells are most gratifying.
But all wondered if it wasn't divided
from itself, and if more sleep hadn't built up on the other side.

XII

Other dreams.
Judy the petulant watered her flowers
from a sprinkling can, and the rose hurtled into bloom.
My message is it's all right to go on, it said.
Sure enough daisies and yellowbirds paired off in the peace of the
    moment,
which is to be lasting, but someone unearthed the old saw
on the gravel beach. "We can't use this." No but we'll go over the top
and down into the wrinkle on the other side, you'll see.
So they did what was natural and becoming, and all were satisfied
and rewarded. And some
shall be excused, and others have to go and wait on the border for it,
if we can believe the poets who wrote all this down many decades ago.
And we should come nearer, it's warmer,
if we want to, only on that other side
which seems so far away from us, but alas is too near
almost to count. With that the hedgerow winked
good-humoredly, and they stand, they stand
unimpressed but interested perhaps
even today, and that's the gist of it.

Dream lover, won't you come to me?
Dream lover, won't you be my darling?
It's not too late or too early.
Dream lover, won't you kiss me and hold me?
Dream lover, won't you miss me and mold me?
See, it was better that the chickens gulped concrete
commas to be able to rinse backwards.
Otherwise the driveling idiots would be maligned
and come to feel transparent.

Dream lover, are you apparent?
I only wish the awful bushel of shins would go away.
My accountant says it's time to harvest the burrs
where the asphalt beaches tame shrieks and the byword is love.

Yet, more and more blobs are in favor of love.
The tax district can't annul it.
The ivy wants to get strenuous.
The old ladies in the tower dream and curse
whoever put them out to pasture with geraniums.

It is too my house.

And they tracked the Canadian trappers far into the mist,
it was gone over with a horsehair comb, brisk
in the seasoned twilight, from which other squall
daffodils and the girls depended. See, it's me.

Briefly the dolls rested on the sink.
If the contest was over, nowhere
had not been told so. Time's evening relish,
hole of the great world, came to ice over
in morning-glory privies where no starlight is,
no autograph sessions, no costume contest.

New creatures fly past, out of the starting gate forever. The pink
     boomerang returns
to home base, flutters, settles in the dust.

Our therapist has been with us for five years.
Some pretty desolate pairing
has gone on in the interval; none of us are satisfied
with that just yet. He scooted down the wind
just in time for us. Omigosh, that means he's here.

Yes, a majestic crash is heading our way.
You and the girls must learn to prize it
while the water buffalo behaves and all is asunder
on the grass, between the chairs, under the apple blossoms.
And what does this have to do with me?
You'd better water your garden again under the circumstances,
look at them till they come down the street,
forming a parade, taut, hangdog. We can run away
at some point? The blue is
materializing and no one will ever know the outcome any more.
No, I mean no one will ever know the outcome,
the sails they took to get here, over fields, marshes,
the salt hay slipping, the season reviving
its forecasts. The sea air is like sludge.
We'll go out and rest in snowbanks while the nightingale titters
and crumbs fall down an airshaft, disappearing forever from view.

If they had heifers on Mars, bub, this would be
all it is like and it would be peaceful in time for mom to go home,
but as it is, we'll have to settle for Siena. As you
can see, the hands of the oversize clock are at 5:30;
the plastrons will be here soon. I forgot
they were coming. I have a handkerchief in this sandwich. Oh, give me
that. The goddam house is haunted,

and you're goofy too. I was only practicing my wail
thought the witch. This really is unfortunate.
Same goes for all the centuries we wafted over to get here,
only to be left in the lurch, far from the nearest poltroon garage,
on a deck dipping roguishly into the foam of the sound.
We should all plan to go back there together
into the room, and count who's there first. By
golly I think she's right. Yes, and you would too,
if a cannonball was your uncle. Yipes,
the general said.

XIII

And some were vortices
of blue, and yellow.
These, wherever the waves grazed, laughingly,
were slower. Then good General Metuchen said, It
has come to my attention some of you are not letting your streamers out.
Please, bear in mind, streamers must be released and parties accompany
    them,
such is my desire. O,
sir, the landgrave said, we cannot do it. Why? Well, we just can't,
that's all. Then I command you to do it. So the plains re-echoed
with indecision that day, and it was a day like the first.

I dream too much, Metuchen swirled, and in the gasps in his doublet
many live fish pirouetted and stank.
Now it was Phoebe's turn to complain: "Whoever thinks he
can outwit the sun is in for a rude awakening. For her parents

are always turning up in the strangest places,
such as the top of a bluff or at a pencil fair,
when fountain pens are the color of crayons dipped in the watercolor that
    was used in the landscape.
We acknowledge it and go on living. This
pen is for you because you're about twenty-four."
Glory how the running of the teams was acknowledged
that day! For they forgot to drain the swamp,
but in doing so created new, higher ground
for kids to live on.
And there was talk of acknowledging it since yesterday:
"It positively shimmers."

Yet how ephemeral are the repercussions, this valley of branches,
when we come to take our place in the parade,
piddling in the foreground, "some in rags,
some in jags, and some in velvet gown," as the saying is,
like that little old Rhode Island lady no one has talked to since last
    November.
I break the silence, it shatters my lips, fronds
come all over me, I am besotted
at least twice this year. Who will lock up their numbers, who'll know
exactly how much we were valued at? Shucks,
the most contented among us are aware of that;
you other buggers can go now. Even with dense night
pouring over us? For how did you expect us to get out
once we got in, or was it a secret for those in authority
to bottle up within us? You did the right thing,
that's for sure. Now it's time to surrender, or be riven asunder, garroted,
    eviscerated
by the actual time of the explosion. They had some nerve

telling us to come over at such and such an hour. I'm sure they'll be sorry
once they've been told about it.
Yes, for this is the season of flares, Farmer Jones will sew a patch on it
until we're delivered. O is it like onions then?
Can it be invisible? But the skunks were swaggering among us but this
    time
it was all a fever, a coming apart at the hinges
glowworms had appeared at, several summers back, before the big naked
cloud pushed rudely into the foreground, and they all sank into apathy,
puzzled by this latest evidence of villainy in the ranks.

How strange it all seems lost! How white it then was! Page torn from a
    notebook . . .
for the end that doesn't come any more.

We so enjoyed having salt to sprinkle on the meat,
until it seemed none of us could be a worker or welfare recipient.
Cashing in on the laughs in the alley,
Melinda strums a thighbone guitar, the rest are off in the distance.
Daytime drowsiness, dizziness, headache, nausea, stomach upset,
    vomiting, diarrhea, lightheadedness, muscle
aches and dry mouth may occur
so long as we are in unreasoning variation to one another,
which might be repaired by dawn's unsealing the tips
of tall buildings, so they sway to and fro,
in time with the maker's rhythm. He had a plan
but it was too late to use it.

Heightened with a sense of mysterious confusion, or completion,
the books in the library give off an odor of display, are about allegorical
    whale-catching,
or about the roads each of us takes, that cross over each other
from here until the end, whichever arrives first.
Yes, Shuffle, he and I many times asked ourselves that,
breaking the theme up
into slivers
that the king melds together, driving in his carriage out of the straight gate
into the taxis of City Hall. Best not to let them guess
what is in your hand. Varmints tell the truth
you may want to sip in later days, which is part of the story, an important
    one,
as is listening to the telegraph
wires, and how we can never listen to nor quite escape the sound
that brings us
to this place of feasting. Again, you've
got to be something without grapes,
and no one knows where it can lead to.
The truant officer plays with a doily,
outside, in the street. Playground noise smears the crowd,
bewitches those who had brought along questions, placating questions of
    faith,

so that when it's all gone a lorn dog's skin
comes quickly up the path, loping into the light of what was done.
My dears, doesn't it all seem a little suspicious to you that we are here,
unable to throw the volleyball into the adjoining courtyard?
Fred the truant officer smiled and turned sheepishly.
It made less difference now,

its fluency was less tortured. So he spoke, and drifted away
out of the girls' thoughts, all but a few of them.

Trevor his dog came, half jumping.
The oblique flute sounded its note of resin.
In time, he said, we all go under the fluted covers
of this great world, with its spiral dissonances,
and then we can see, on the other side,
what rascals are up to. What games the malevolent play.
Only then we are distanced, and can relax in the great
cradle of earth's two cents, for what it's worth,
and can recline, looking upward to the great here and there,
even as it falls short at our feet.

I'll go you one better, Fred chimed in, here's a diver,
let's call her Josephine, who dives and dives, further and downward,
all our lives' span, to the basis of that bridge.
Does that make her any more coquettish than we are? More sure-footed?
No but and here's what I was going to say
all along, must we recast ourselves in the image of the ocean floor:
To wit, are we not shipshape entities? Have we not corollas?
O the moon shines bright on the birdbath
as on a summer's stream, and we pass slowly from view,
borne by the tide's single-mindedness, and come to seem happy
as birds frolic, words wuther, and the contented are at peace again.

Whoa, Trevor responded, these dances of life—
always pissing, and shitting, and waking up in the great grapefruit
as in a trundle bed, breathless following how it goes, leads
to the great here and there.

35

Let's take my toes, if you insist. What I said
no one now remembers. Oh, but I do, Josephine said brightly.

We were talking about thingamabobs, and how one sheep's antler
can subdue dispassionate multitudes with its glint.
But is that all that brought us together? What about sex?
Yes, he remembers quietly, we too were part of the line.
Then why have sidled against this puzzle-wall for miles and miles?
Do you think it can speak to us?
Or are we, as was said of the others, just slush?

Hold it, I have an idea, Fred groaned. Now some of you, five at least, must
     go over in that little shack.
I'll follow with the tidal waves, and we'll see what happens next.

It was agreed for that day they would separate into two groups,
the lovers and learners side by side with the vexed and disinherited.
If only his plan had worked better—
but we must learn to read, "and that ain't easy," Trevor summarized.
Oh for a pen, for a blotter,
for a more regulated environment. Tired, the girls lay down to sleep amid
     the rocks.
It was just play, they dreamed,
tomorrow will be another day, and different.
For after taking off from the spring, the squirrels
touch earth again and die. Much that is lovely
may be voiced then, though not exclusively. The mad neighbor
pursues a fish; desperate, islands collapse,
and it's all vertigo now on the railroad. Yes, chained

to a post, I might have agreed with that. But now, the bees
come. See how fast they come,
suspecting the glad harbor holds opals for them.
But the wish for truth is denied. A twinkly Christmas tree
rushes over the sand, and whether the scale is practiced for the benefit of
    many,
or whether it voices a portent of shooting stars to come
is not known. I'll write you from that solemn coast,
but you must promise never to remember me, never speak of me,
until we are found at last behind the bathroom door, with the broom.

XV

Fred began to get chills: It sure was his mission, he averred,
to get everyone out before the avalanche came down.
But it was equally certain the girls' light chatter had dispersed
the whaling ships to wherever. In tints of prune, or lilac, these arrived
to chase the gloom of our arrival. Now, some of them were still in short
    pants.
But all that mattered was that they take off their clothes
in innocence, miming sleep, and be none too particular.
"The chime irritates me, I'll lose the thread
if I follow it much further," Trevor whispered. And where
should we go for relief, we who have never had any, have never felt
what it means to go without pangs, unless momentarily forgotten,
by the bridge, in sunlight's vale? It's because there are pairs of everything,
    that we miss the
chink in the stair where memory was supposed to reside. Indeed,
she was there until recently, until this morning; no one could say
why she went away.

*　　*　　*

The consignment of leeches hadn't arrived yet.

I was whispering, where were you?
I know, I was close by, but dared not speak. Try surrendering,
but not often. A loved one may be driving home
into the forest and then this—it's enough to make you ache
with hunger at a banquet.

The men never learned to love much. There was both hunger and sadness
at their feasting, the rocks wave over the airstrip, the hyenas of sleep
    redescend,
the leeches brace themselves for one last fetid leap into thanksgiving
there where loam signals the synod's pallid approach. It was a little too
    unresonant.
Still, they'd imagined they'd be saved
all this time, so why take a different tack now?
So marl oozed through the bookshelves
and a yellow wind turned the trailer park to dust.
Strange glyphs seemed to advise one to consign oneself to temporary
    oblivion;
we were very expressive in words, and in feeling. The mastodon broke his
    chain
and wanted to be petted, or at least encouraged, and tall lupine
clambered up the pesky wall, infesting projects with smug I-told-you-so's
in case any of us were still rattling around inside the domed hut's
    emptiness.
I like it here, but why should anybody else? It was my spasm that brought
    this on,

now I'll sink or swim in it. The latter, preferably,
but Damian still reached for Emily's shoelaces,
as the lich-gate came unhooked. It was still laughing like a lunatic
several hours later when reinforcements arrived at the stockade
just as General Forester's nerves were giving out, and a thin gruel
was being served to the men in the guise of supper. "I'll not swallow this!"
But you must, otherwise the story would have no turning,
and blind sockets gaze at streaks the plow left
in sunburnt earth, for only some are permitted to be happy,
surmised Emily, and that means none of us
at the present time. Sure enough, Trevor leaped on the horizon,
causing cheerfulness to jump-start the stubborn little band of marauders.
　　When they awoke,
as from a dream, only a mauve magician was occupying the premises,
and he too pretended not to notice anything was amiss. This was too much
　　for
Laure. She pushed impatiently past the guards, on the pretext
of bringing Trevor his bowl and saucer, secretly
counting up the number of clothespins that still lay scattered around the
　　tent threshold.
This marks the moment

when everything must be summed up or there will no longer be a way past
　　the mercenaries.
You see we all thought the ride would be lovely
and worth the trip, which it was, but now we cannot go anywhere
having already been everywhere. No, do you
understand how realistic it all is? Bear-baiting was considered a privilege
in those days. Then I have one piece of advice for you: Go easy
on the imperatives, for night is coming, than which there will be none
　　bigger.

Sure enough, suds coursed down the boulder's slate face,
moonflowers danced, and it was all here and in a jiffy,
the present, made up like a cadaver, but more tastefully, though not too
much so. A raft descended the millrace
and Lou jumped off at the prearranged moment,
to the astonishment of many, but survived to yodel another day.
We listened to some semiclassical music, and someone got the idea of
      hooking up
the car's old engine to the plaster sheep on the hill.
The effect was startling; moths buzzed in the light
from its extraordinary vibrations. Fifteen years passed in this way.
When it was over no one had the courage to come out into the daylight,
or knew there was any. I fell asleep
on a sandhill, and dreamed this, and gave it to you, and you thanked me,
      solemnly,
but we were not permitted to associate, only to correspond, and you came
      out
to me again, and we wished one another good afternoon, and then went
      away
again into the fog-lit embrasure. Not that we didn't have good reason
to do whatever we did, but the question never came up again.
Where was I? Back in the explorer's cottage, with the thundering sea
bathing the rafters, not sure how many of us were to have gone out to meet
the pack of returning travelers. Some stayed behind. Others felt it a
      breach of dignity
to have gone. Still others put a good face on it, and were in turn
kissed by blue bats, and the coroner caught up on his sleep. "Forty winks!
That's all they allowed me!" And grumbling, he too left the shift.
For wasn't that what the Creator had in mind? That we should all muck
      about
helplessly, for a few minutes, and then stand back
to look at what a small difference we had made merely by observing crusty
      silence and then speaking up briefly?

Sure as canvasbacks are part of nature, we could not have observed it
another way, or brought our chairs back to where the laundry was spread
   out, effectively drying.

XVI

Dolores . . . you wisteria . . .
Destined to be destined
Like a lilac I am coming on your shoe.
Uncle Margaret was dull-witted.
He had tried the various positions.
The tame suburban landscape excited him.
He had met his match.
Dimples replaced the mollusk with shoe-therapy.
Sun burning his way through that flower . . .

Since Labor Day hardly any curls were outside
on the ladies' heads, the ones who sold jelly-bean screwdrivers inside.
Uncle Margaret's wren ranch was getting on his nerves just now.
Why, I'll wager some of them even wear raccoon coats
on shopping tours to East Testicle, he thundered. But what does showing
   off prove,
except to stop it, right here and now?
                                        Aw, don't
be such a grouch, Dimples curdled, but then suddenly the plain was
   awash with
ocher sediment; testaments to the superiority of life overflowed the trap;
all around us were boondoggles and poverty parades.
Which is it to be? Shall I spoil you
a little, or can we just go back to being peacemakers

in love, and in our time? Broken clocks
sound the hour in forty different cities at once, and in this, I was right,
I told you so, Jane's warlock said. But in other things I am less right,
like wanting to go in to town the fast way.
Yes you surely are right:
Some dream, some faint away, others are dragged up in morning's
    consciousness
like breakers from overseas. The shore patrol, ditchdiggers clawing,
and the mostly interesting ephemera of dawn, then a big one,
then a not so big one, then another one, then quite a small one,
then another big one followed by two middle-sized ones. For whom
are these? Day struts and stammers
on our headlands, so it seems, half-threatening to be off into night
as all collapses, leaving the players in fearful jeopardy,
but as time goes on they begin to forget their bruises,
settling down into the seats of the jalopy of day.

What if someone called back to you
from a distance? What would that sound like? What would you think?
    Does anyone
care any more about it's being night? "We think
night is fine, it enables one to get over the headaches of day
and so survive until day returns,
a limpet in his arms, one blue eye poking out from the vellum of his
    matted hair."
So what is important,
if the universe decides not to challenge us, and even breakwaters fall
    asleep?
Why, the old, seminal
undertow, that's what. The nor'easter will be out in force tomorrow,
an insane force in an otherwise docile universe.

Why beat about the bush? One of us knows the truth, and she isn't telling.
And so they betook themselves to the Carolinas.

Now he was the daughter or granddaughter of somebody famous,
folks for miles around knew that. But no one could say what she was up to,
she was far too clever for that. "Look, Uncle Wilmer," she'd say sometimes.
"The dark forest is my kitty. Just feel how soft it is!"
Let chunky Ida have that, Uncle thought, but he said nothing.
The tides were still active, one coming in
as another was going out, and one's thinking got caught
in these shifts, too positive some days, too blank the next,
and it all did matter somehow, though it didn't seem to
compute at any given moment. Pink shrouds fell on the pansy jamboree,
mocking the circular nature of events with its own kind of back-to-the-
    beginning
free fall. A few pansies got drowned. Yet this was as nothing to the terrible
muttering of the distant cavalry, like an express train coming to exhaust
    itself on the shore,
and over and over the same note was struck. Go back! This is a place too far.
In any case you ought to reconsider the places back there,
teeming with sandalwood and bees. You think you know it
but you don't, there are inner coasts to be discovered, sat on,
whittled to a point more dangerous than Father Time's tuning fork,
if you but knew. In the minute
before the terrible tide turns there's time enough to go back
if you are engaged, shoes slushy with sand.
Go, do as I say.
                    Uncle Bert chided the fens at Mr.
McPlaster's side, and they stretched away into the hyacinth distance,
    meek enough,
or so it was thought, for the time being. Then everything began to explode

in a geyser of impatience that crested at where the nearest cloud-scraps
   had been.
"Now that's funny,
he was here only a moment ago. I thought I saw him go up, and out." The
   flies
on the flypaper said they hadn't seen him; birds whistled unconsciously
at a shadow-bulge in the grass that could have been almost anything
except the two principal survivors, who were nowhere to be found
on a fine day, with the red mailbox standing near, as always, *if you know
   what I mean.*
This is where we break for lunch.
Those who want to go back to the base camp can do so. I swear
I've never seen a more ornery bunch, though civic-minded
at heart, I suppose, but there's a great gap between their intentions
and the harvest moon that seems to belie mediocre aspirations
even as it secretly promotes them, waxes as it wanes
into delirium tremens, and other missed opportunities
too numerous to scramble for, in disbelief's fomented ocean.
Oh my there were a lot of them
then, some as had names, and these were brought to the front of the group,
with Ida, who seemed to be their leader.
Roll back this pokey late-morning sense of being extra,
she was begged. Bring us all to your birch tree.

XVII

After a few rounds of this the leader fell silent.

Well, what did you want me to do,
arrest the perpetrators?

What would we have seen?
Ida and the rest imaged the tambourine. They were never to start.
In fact as they got older, wasps reminded them continually
of their delicate condition; they never amounted to much
and were called up for screening. Well sir, sure as your nose
heads north, an' they were caught out in the singing sands
a hundred miles from home. And decimated.

You see the mouse was in between the papers.
There was a limit to what any fool could do.
Our faces were wiped clean, we wept for the goodness
that is earth, and in autumn comes to fondle us
with new, rich, more mature colors, just as the sun is going down
and down and down for the last time. Night did not recognize us
or our claims, but the night season is good
for all and sundry, to children especially, and plays a game without brains.
In the utopian schemes there was nothing left. Some resolutions
perhaps? Maybe a little freedom for play? That was all right,
but time was up, which was the same as if there was no way,
no bemused situation to chortle at, no lava
on the red earth's rim, which is running down to meet the land and the sea
in a way that deviates. O say is there any more,
truly? Can we have something? No, the machinery is ugly and preserved
    in dust.
There were no two ways to have it. All came undone
from Brigitte's shorts, and this was supposed to be the way home,
even. But not anything mattered any more, not even to the shirts
some children wore then, out of sight until the last tide destroys us.
The envy of the age sweeps over us, tidying us into pits of darkness
that men shall understand, and forgive their promises
to those who had forgotten them, lauding all future dust-storms
as long as the king will stay alive on the road.

Bird-feeders introduced a new element of sashaying
nobody picked up on, and the direction all were taking was done to death
most slovenly. Where the girls' shorts
had been, only a minus sign stood.
So the bad angels went away, and other creatures returned.

XVIII

Did you read that book I was telling you about? Ach, it concerns puberty.
Do you suffer, child? That is fundamentally inaccurate.
Your talents are warehoused now. In another time they would spring forth
with the red beacons of spring, prepared to do battle with rocks.
In a tenderer meridian
their phalanxes would cripple the overseers, bonk.
The guides would unleash their elastic trains.
So much sorrow, yet quite a lot of laughter. "I say,
Does the train run on Sundays?" We, quite a lot of us, were mired east of
    here
and could feel the valley's separateness and shortcomings. When it came
    time to repeat
the scene, Dennis was numb with fear.
His velvet tread was steadfast on the stair. The fall had occurred
to someone nice this time, tatters of milk on the stone.
Preserve us all from horseradish
but if the saints won't let us in, blast us
into nether pandemonium, for that will be where their compacted truths
    hibernate.

See, they need to have a story line. Sexy. So it appears.
The seven colors are remanded. We should have put aside our differences.

We are refracted. They never learn to drive.
They never slide much
these days,
what with the cartwheel hats, and all the underachievers.
It's a big scare. The Lollipop Mountains are an entertainment mogul.
She said. But—
they are under orders. When the balls came on Fred was over with the
    bears. He started.
They all did waiting for something coherent to happen.
Then it was all over.
The ball-juice had expired
in the lobby, as though something were promised me that came out like an
    anteater,
poked around, went back in.

Slush and feathers. The hippo trod on a pine needle, they all sank back
    into relief.
Everywhere we go is something to eat
and fat disappointment, tears in the rain. Somebody is coming over the
    radio.
A lull.

XIX

He complicated everything by dying. He wouldn't hear
of it. Fate was two valleys away. Wind slithered over the sandbar. Two
    women caught the train
from the new town. More elaborate buildings betokened sly adjustments
in the retinue of the living, underground. Aphasia leaked,
a sprinkle of diamond confetti, over confused lands and places,

the places we had ignored when we went through them the last time
when you were there for me.
                          I pointed the ladder to the ceiling.
It seemed we could join there.
The pre-Columbian bats were in ferment, just at that period.
The ladder shrinks in living water
whereas in your time the fiction we would otherwise be without
stays and stays and finally comes to seem permanent,
all along. It was almost twenty to six,
they churred. Slim weasels stirred behind the chink,
the oxymoron got his rocks off, there was hell to pay, but pay it they did,
after which the streets absorbed the laughter and lust that had been the
    morning
as Pamela was at last captured.

XX

A virtual rout ensued. Tell me, can you tell it any
different where you come from? I know the highlights are blurred
now, the witnesses less than forthcoming,
but fences are down, and we can travel where it was never supposed
anyone could go, to highlands of the spirit that refresh and punish
the blame we were supposed to ingest, until they leave that off, too.
A ton of regret is supplied and it never needs any replenishing,
as long as we citizens still stomp the earth, favor it with our occasional
attention and pull up stakes each night. But I'm not too sure what boils at
    the center of the earth.

I'll go along with what you say. We must isolate the moment
from its comperes, look behind it,

and if possible draw the appropriate conclusions from its appearance of
   unease
while the nurses are still on the grounds. The fat clock ticks. It's time to
   repair
to the orchard, or just to repair.

When it was all over, a sheep emerged from inside the house.
A cheer went up, for it was recognized that these are lousy times
to be living in, yet we do live in them:
We are the case.
And seven times seven ages later it would still be the truth in
   appearances,
festive, eternal, misconstrued. Does anyone still want to play?

It was only inevitable, after all,
what shoes they could muster. So they made bold. Prudence won the
   spelling bee with "cotoneaster."
Harry wanted to believe. Prodding succeeds. So does popularity. Pierre
   thought it might too.
Lochinvar believed. All systems became taut. This is only what they did
   do.

They danced, and became meaningful to each other. It was cosmic time,
tasting of grit. If this is a mutual admiration society,
why not? We were, after all, going to pull our town out of the encampment.
   The proud similarities
twinkle. Coming back to our doorstep, it was in the vegetables' vocabulary
and nobody had noticed. Nobody, that is, except Swann.
Anyway, it overshoots the mark, as a log a waterfall.
Each gemstone blooms out of corruption, and somebody knows it.

But if that is the case, who knows it? Bookcases wouldn't give you the
   time of day.
Time wasted in beehives is about right. And extraneous moraines,
coming from the kitchen to be all over the map of the United States,
and Canada, whose states are affectionately known as "provinces."
Aye, to be brought up in the provinces equals an old Dodge or De Soto,
and who is coming back to get us, after all? Looks lonesome,
I mean. Where's the energy needed to strike?

Come, it's silver, children, the unbearable letdown
has gone under the hill to bide its time. Centuries shall pass away this
   way.
When we wake up it will be over. The motor will have started up,
and peas have been planted in Wyoming. Time grabs us
again, it's terrible, for a little while. And then it becomes more and more
   like this
in its way. Then time broke off
discussions, they were shunted to Sheboygan, some mystery wolf came to
   the appointment
instead, there were further negotiations, a child lay dying, there was more
   other
to be sad over, the whistle charged doom, its impact
was tremendous, light exploded all over the football field, the nails were
   there,
pus of the sun, brooding, help, it looks more doctrinaire, than we can
   handle, I mean,
and goes on and on, not just changing in the fire
from the attic bathroom. Kids came over, it wasn't right to put the blame
   on anyone,
can you see, it should have gotten by all right, but it didn't, that's what
   "hopeless"

is all about, where I come from, oh you shan't, shall you, shut up, the dish,
over
what I am doing is all broke out, the cattails
again, more underwear, trees implored, then lunch, for crying out loud,
and more of the same, ideal limits, a good spanking. Call your jewels up,
it seems the only way.
Who am I to be horsing around? You are someone. Rats. A tan umbrella
coasted.

Weary, the dogs broke off the game.

It was just dandy where you were standing.
It was like everywhere. It was just average.

XXI

When more and more people come to you, you know
what they are saying, and you know how to deal with them.
Many were the whiskers that applied that day,
and many the salvage operations bent on rejecting them.
If you have some ointment it would be good to use it
now. Otherwise the opportunity may never again present itself.
I know you mean well, Hopeful murmured. Talkative was
starting to tell one of his stories again, and smiling,
Hopeful silently abetted it. He knew the old boy was feeling his oats,
which was fine with him, as he too was feeling good. Talkative, you old so-
and-so, he volunteered. Then his father-in-law blew up. The Overall Boys,
fishing poles in hand,

charged into nether regions.

Susie never thought she'd see the day when so much surplus was at stake,
and she alone, outdoors, waiting for the postman's red bicycle
for what seemed like ages. He explained that it was a routine
    assassination,
that that was what had delayed him. Crestfallen, Susie hardly dared look up
into the eyes of her man, a breeze was blowing, it was snowing. The
    droplets made diagonal streaks in the air
where pterodactyls had been. It was time for an exodus of sorts;
Paul picked up the legend
                              where it had been broken off: "No
blame accrues to those who were left behind, unless, haply, they were
    climbing
the wall to get a better view of the stars, in which case the next-to-last
must pay a tribute, and so on. It can be anything, old money,
a calico scarf, whatever has soiled the hand of the donor by staying
to wear out its welcome. O in time it will shrivel.
What is it to imagine something you had forgotten once, is it
inventing, or more of a restoration from ancient mounds that were
    probably there?
You that can tell all, tell this."

At first Talkative was reluctant to speak, then the words fell
like spring rain from his lips, all was as it had been before,
with no two dancers in step, and a bright, really bright light exploded
above the barn. A horse wanders away
and is abruptly inducted into the carousel,
eyes flying, mane askew. There is no end to the dance,
even death pales in comparison, and at the same time we are forced to
take into account the likelihood of the moment's behaving badly, the
    eventual cost
to our side in terms of dignity, compromised integrity. Twelve princesses

stepped ashore, no one knew them, they too seemed not to know where
    they were.
"In what region . . ." one began timidly, then the whole flock took off
like a shout, leaving the beleaguered ground to fend for itself.
"There were picture books at that time,
and dreams woven in and out of them. But one was not to notice,
only to go on behaving. And at the end, when everything was added up,
we probably owed them a penny. It's enough to make you weep.
But skies are gilded and armored, we shall put a brave face

"on it for a time, then school will be over, and sublime rest
flow from the uncorked flask like a prodigious perfume,
or sleep, a potent but dangerous brew,
a new assignment. Then we can get out of hock,
redeem Daddy's dear old coupons." He broke off, not wanting to bestir
the others, who had in fact ceased to hear, so monotonous
was the noise of his voice, like rain that flails the spears of vetch
in Maytime, to reap a tiny investment.
So we faced the new day,
like a pilgrim who sees the end of his journey deferred forever.
Who could predict where we would be led, to what
extremes of aloneness? Yet the horizon is civil.

A struggle ensued and the driver fell out of the vehicle.
And what did the old lady do then?
"She gave them some broth, without any bread, and . . . and . . ."

All are like soup.

*   *   *

So if it pleases you to come
out we all await thy pleasure, Stuart Hofnagel.
Who was with Young Topless? It seemed then an abyss was forming,
a new set of lagoons. More than look past it
one cannot, for more
than that is denied us.
So have I heard it said in old kingdoms, it said.
Larkspur towering over miniature turrets. The bandoleer was shot to hell.

The spa looked closed. So,
if you are in the market for a steeple, I commend this one
rigorously. It was not given to human divination to exhume it
like the comet, but to pause briefly, the blind
man's praise will cook itself. A giant paw
over the moon. Melons bloomed in corners. Shrimp blew away
to be fecund elsewhere, next year.
In time it will be your caesura too, but we mustn't
think of that. We caregivers especially. We must forget,
while others only live, peer into circles of living embroidery. The geese
will jump for you again, anon. Then it's no business. They closed
the place, the food court, they all
have gone away, it's restless, and mighty, as an ark
to the storm, yet the letter
of the law is obeyed, and sometimes the spirit
in forgotten tales of the seekers—O who were they?
Mary Ann, and Jimmy—no, but who were they?
Who have as their mantles on the snow
and we shall never reach land
before dark, yet who knows what advises them,
discreet in the mayhem? And then it's bright in the defining pallor of their
    day.

Does this clinch anything? We were cautioned once, told not to venture
   out—
yet I'd offer this much, this leaf, to thee.
Somewhere, darkness churns and answers are riveting,
taking on a fresh look, a twist. A carousel is burning.
The wide avenue smiles.